ESTATE PUBLICATIONS

BEDFORDSHIRE

Street maps with index
Administrative Districts
Population Gazetteer
Road Map with index
Postcodes

COUNTY RED BOOKS
This atlas is intended for those requiring street maps of the historical and commercial centres of towns within the county. Each locality is normally presented on one or two pages and although, with many small towns, this space is sufficient to portray the whole urban area, the maps of large towns and cities are for centres only and are not intended to be comprehensive. Such coverage in Super and Local Red Books (see page 2).

Every effort has been made to verify the accuracy of information in this book but the publishers cannot accept responsibility for expense or loss caused by any error or omission. Information that will be of assistance to the user of these maps will be welcomed.

The representation of a road, track or footpath on the maps in this atlas is no evidence of the existence of a right of way.

Street plans prepared and published by ESTATE PUBLICATIONS, Bridewell House, TENTERDEN, KENT. The Publishers acknowledge the co-operation of the local authorities of towns represented in this atlas.

Ordnance Survey® This product includes mapping data licensed from Ordnance Survey® with the permission of the Controller of Her Majesty's Stationery Office.

COUNTY RED BOOK

BEDFORDSHIRE

contains street maps for each town centre

SUPER & LOCAL RED BOOKS

are street atlases with comprehensive local coverage

BEDFORD

including: Bromham, Clapham, Great Barford, Kempston, Oakley, Willington, Wootton etc.

LUTON & DUNSTABLE

including: Barton-le-Clay, Caddington, Harlington, Houghton Regis, Toddington etc.

MILTON KEYNES

including: Buckingham, Bletchley, Leighton Buzzard, Hanslope, Yardley Gobion, Deanshanger etc.

CONTENTS

LEGEND TO STREET MAPS

One-Way Street	→	Post Office	●
Pedestrianized	▨	Public Convenience	Ⓒ
Car Park	Ⓟ	Place of Worship	+

Scale of street plans: 4 Inches to 1 mile (unless otherwise stated on the map).

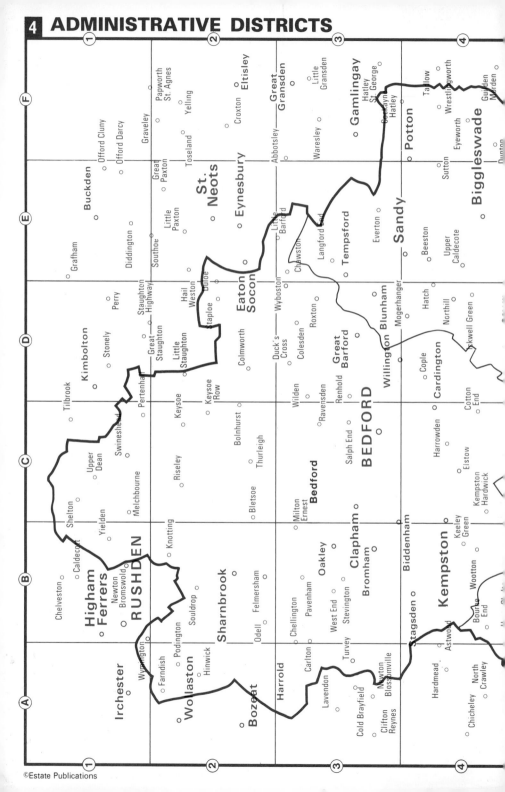

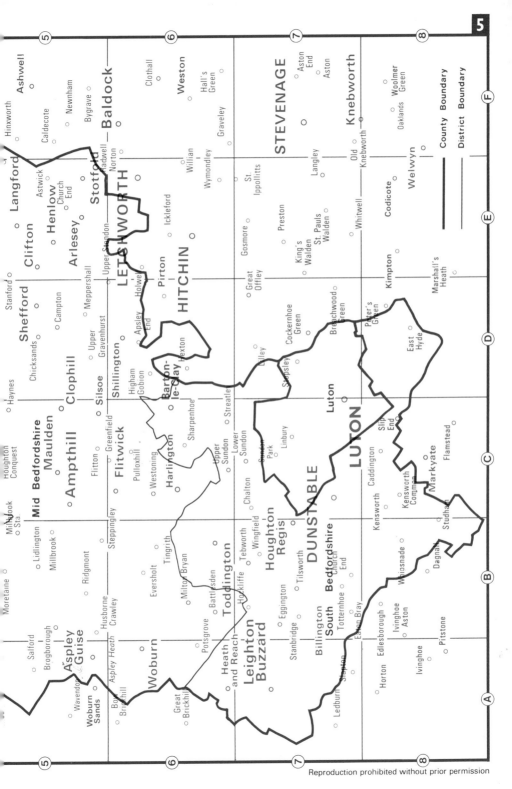

5

GAZETTEER INDEX TO ROAD MAP
with populations
County of Bedfordshire population **540,004**

Districts:

Luton	**171,671**
Mid Bedfordshire	**125,700**
North Bedfordshire	**133 692**
South Bedfordshire	**108,941**

Ampthill **7,240**	9 C5	Duloe	8 D2
Apsley End	9 D6	Dunstable **32,845**	9 B7
Arlesey **4,940**	9 E5	Dunton **660**	8 F4
Aspley Guise **2,360**	9 A5		
Aspley Heath **560**	*	Eastcotts **1,871**	*
Astwick **30**	9 E5	Eaton Bray **2,367**	9 B8
		Edworth **70**	9 F5
Barton-le-Clay **3,488**	9 C6	Eggington **275**	9 B7
Battlesden **40**	9 B6	Elstow **616**	8 C4
Bedford **133,692**	8 C3	Eversholt **390**	9 B6
Beeston	8 E4	Everton **540**	8 E3
Biddenham **1,241**	8 B3	Eyeworth **100**	8 F4
Biggleswade **15,250**	8 E4		
Billington **425**	9 A7	Farndish	8 A1
Bletsoe **246**	8 B2	Felmersham **752**	8 B2
Blunham **1,020**	8 D3	Flitton & Greenfield **1,310**	9 C5
Bolnhurst & Keysoe **674**	8 C2	Flitwick **12,350**	9 C6
Bourne End	8 A4		
Brogborough **330**	9 A5	Gravenhurst **620**	9 D5
Bromham **3,909**	8 B3	Great Barford **1,754**	8 D3
Broom	9 E5	Greenfield & Flitton **1,083**	9 C6
Caddington & Slip End **5,620**	9 C8	Harlington **2,380**	9 C6
Campton & Chicksands **1,790**	9 D5	Harrold **1,143**	8 A2
Cardington **255**	8 C4	Harrowden	8 C4
Carlton & Chellington **911**	8 A3	Hatch	8 D4
Chalgrave **455**	*	Haynes **1,090**	9 C5
Chalton	9 C7	Heath & Reach **1,340**	9 A7
Chawston	8 E3	Henlow **3,170**	9 E5
Chicksands & Campton **2,332**	9 D5	Higham Gobion	9 D6
Church End, Arlesey	9 E5	Hinwick	8 A2
Church End, Dunstable	9 B7	Hockliffe **721**	9 B7
Clapham **3,501**	8 B3	Holwell	9 E6
Clifton **2,840**	9 E5	Houghton Conquest **1,420**	9 C5
Clophill **1,820**	9 C5	Houghton Regis **16,104**	9 B7
Cockayne Hatley &		Hulcote & Salford **210**	9 A5
Wrestlingworth **840**	8 F3	Husborne Crawley **270**	9 A6
Colesden	8 D3	Hyde **407**	9 D8
Colmworth **381**	8 D2		
Cople **761**	8 D4	Ickwell Green	8 D4
Cotton End	8 C4		
Cranfield **5,100**	9 A5	Keeley Green	8 B4
		Kempston **8,323**	8 B4
Dean & Shelton **378**	8 C1	Kempston Hardwick	8 C4
Ducks Cross	8 D2	Kempston Rural **1,193**	*

6

Kensworth **1,584**	9 B8
Kensworth Common	9 C8
Keysoe & Bolnhurst **674**	8 C2
Keysoe Row	8 C2
Knotting & Souldrop **259**	8 B1

Langford **3,030**	9 E5
Langford End	8 E3
Leighton-Linslade **32,610**	9 A7
Lidlington **1,310**	9 B5
Limbury **9,455**	9 C7
Little Barford **33**	8 E2
Little Staughton **443**	8 D2
Lower Shelton	8 B4
Luton **171,671**	9 C8

Marston Moretaine **4,020**	9 B5
Maulden **3,010**	9 C5
Melchbourne & Yielden **312**	8 B1
Meppershall **1,670**	9 D5
Millbrook **140**	9 B5
Millbrook Sta	9 B5
Milton Bryan **130**	9 B6
Milton Ernest **636**	8 B3
Mogerhanger **700**	8 D3

| Northill **2,430** | 8 D4 |

Oakley **2,375**	8 B3
Odell **258**	8 A2
Old Warden **170**	8 D4

Pavenham **672**	8 B3
Pertenhall **226**	8 C1
Podington **369**	8 A2
Potsgrove **40**	9 A6
Potton **4,620**	8 F4
Pulloxhill **910**	9 C6

Ravensden **665**	8 C3
Renhold **1,126**	8 C3
Ridgmont **450**	9 B5
Riseley **1,329**	8 C2
Roxton **1,245**	8 D3

Salford & Hulcote **190**	9 E5
Salph End	8 C3
Sandy **11,400**	8 E3
Sharnbrook **1,984**	8 B2
Sharpenhoe	9 C6
Shefford **5,140**	9 D5

Shelton & Dean **378**	8 C1
Shillington **1,930**	9 D6
Silsoe **1,690**	9 C5
Silver End, Haynes	9 D5
Slip End & Caddington **5,620**	9 C8
Souldrop & Knotting **259**	8 B2
Southill **1,130**	9 D5
Stagsden **365**	8 B4
Stanbridge **728**	9 A7
Stanford	9 D5
Staploe **346**	8 D2
Steppingley **220**	9 B6
Stevington **572**	8 B3
Stewartby **982**	8 C4
Stondon **1,830**	9 E6
Stopsley **9,472**	9 D7
Stotfold **6,680**	9 E5
Streatley **634**	9 C7
Studham **1,200**	9 B8
Sundon **493**	9 C6
Sundon Park **10,522**	9 C7
Sutton **319**	8 F4
Swineshead **144**	8 C1

Tebworth	9 B7
Tempsford **560**	8 E3
Thurleigh **617**	8 C2
Tilsworth **343**	9 B7
Tingrith **150**	9 B6
Toddington **4,500**	9 B7
Totternhoe **1,312**	9 B8
Turvey **1,083**	8 A3

| Upper Caldecote | 8 E4 |
| Upper Shelton | 8 B4 |

West End	8 B3
Westoning **2,110**	9 C6
Whipsnade **497**	9 B8
Wilden **429**	8 C3
Willington **797**	8 D3
Wilshamstead (Wilstead) **2,341**	8 C4
Wingfield	9 B7
Woburn **1,020**	9 A6
Wootton **3,765**	8 B4
Wrestlingworth & Cockayne Hatley **840**	8 F4
Wyboston	8 E2
Wymington **865**	8 A1

| Yielden & Melchbourne **312** | 8 B1 |

Population figures are based upon the 1991 census and relate to the local authority area or parish as constituted at that date. Some figures have been updated from the 1999 Estimates & Forecasts Document produced by Bedfordshire County Council. Places with no population figure form part of a larger local authority area or parish. District boundaries are shown on pages 4-5.

Population figures in bold type.

*Parish not shown on map pages 8-9 due to limitation of scale

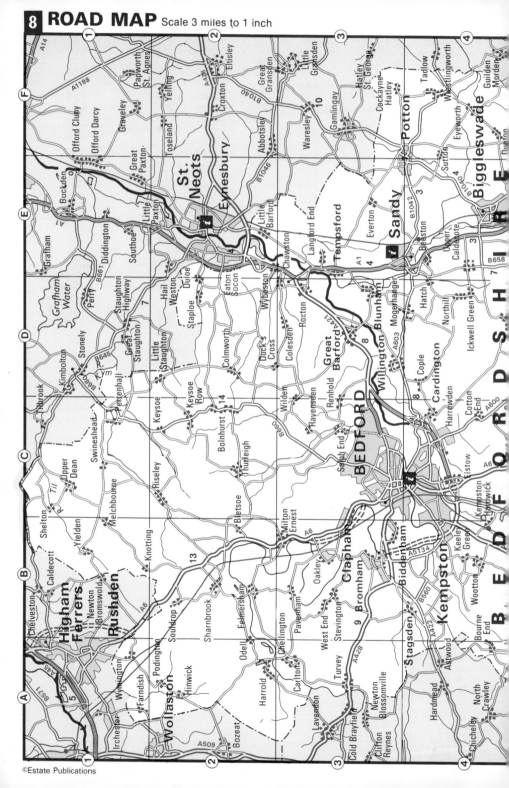

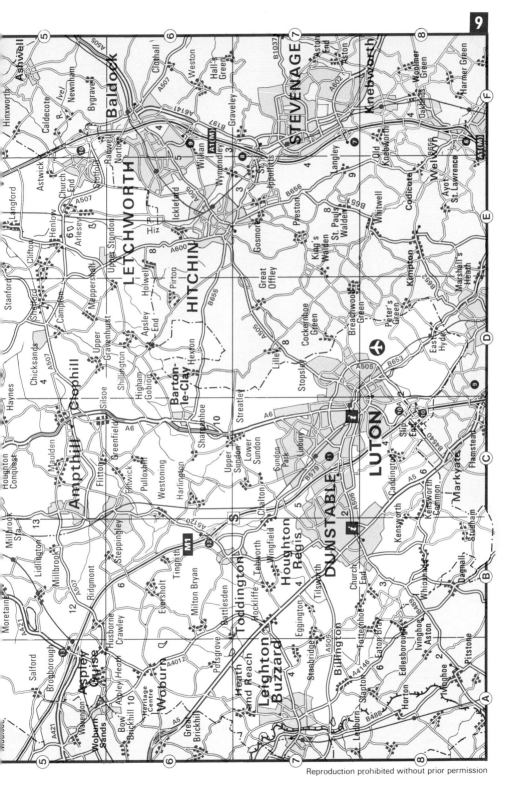

9

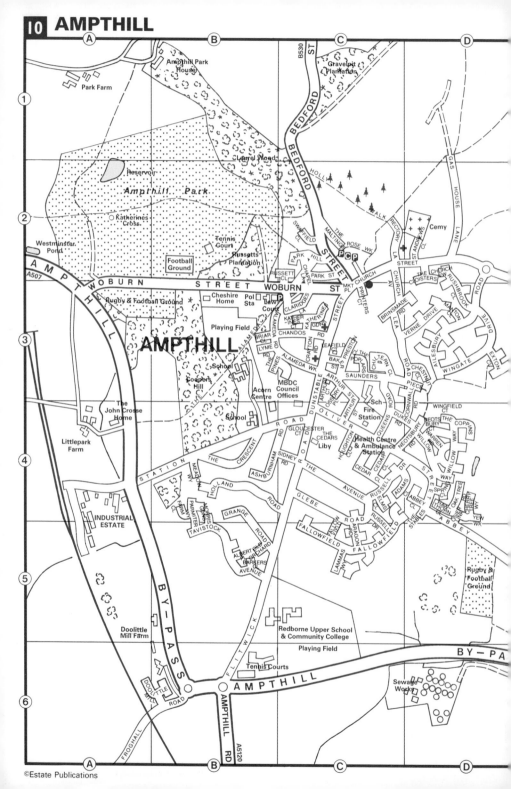

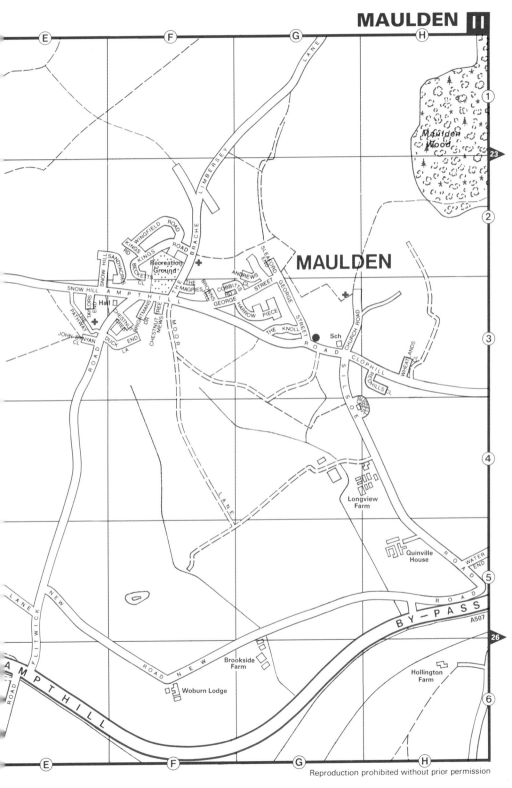

MAULDEN

Maulden Wood

Recreation Ground

Hall

Longview Farm

Quinville House

Brookside Farm

Woburn Lodge

Hollington Farm

BY-PASS   A507

A B C D

A6

1

CUT THROAT LA

Supermarke

Golf Course

Me
Ce

Playing
Fields
The Alexander
Sports Centre

WINDMILL HILL

B R O M H A M

Club House

Playing
Fields

A428

DEEP

GOLDEN CT
LAVENHAM DR
LEE CL
PL

MACREE

HOWDEN GDNS
WOODLUCAS

QUEENS CL

NEVERN GDNS

SPINNEY
DEEP

LANE

BROMHAM ROAD

BEVERLEY GROVE

CHESTERTON MEWS MAINE ROW

SIDNEY

2

SPINNEY

POWER
JOHNSON

ELGER CL

TURN

R O A D

BROMH

Biddenham

THORPE CT
FRANKLYN GDNS

HAMPDEN CT

DUCK END LA

GOLD

LANE

School

NODDERS AV

DARLOW

DRIVE

St Gregory's
Middle School

BEVERLEY CRES

FOX
GLOVES

CUTCLIFFE PL
CUTCLIFFE
ALL SAINTS RD
GDNS

HOSP

M A I N

CHURCH END

VICARS

DAYS

REGENTS MEWS

THE PADDOCK

ISON

B I D D E N H A M

R O A D

Biddenham
Upper School

GRO WEST

WESTFIELD RD

WINIFRED

COVENTRY

PREST

3

MANOR RD

CLOSE

OLD OAKS DR

Queens Park

Schools

School

MARLBOROUGH

WESTBOURNE

IDDE

Golf Course

ST MELLION DR

Bedford
Hockey
Centre

Westfield
School

Schools

Recreation
Ground

CARLISLE RD

CHESTER RD
OLDFIELD
GDNS

CHESTNUT RD
ALLEN RD
HANTHORNE AV
LA BURNUM AV

BOYD GDNS
SAUNDERS RD

KELEY AV

WINGFIELD

ROAD

ST PAULS RD
TRINITY RD

SHORT RD

AVENUE

4

CARLISLE RD

OUSELAND RD

FORD COLS RD

+

River Great Ouse

O L D
WROXHM
WY

RANWORTH

MARTHAM

FORD WY

HICKLING CL

ORMESBY

WESBY

HONEY END

OUSE

WOODSTOCK

Queen

5

KINGSWOOD WAY

PORTWAY

GREAT

WOODVILLE DR

SANDERS

CHAPMAN

GILBERT

MORTIMER RD

EARL HOME

JACEY CT

DENTON

H I L L G R O U N D S

VIKING GRO

DRIVE

KINGSTON

RIPON CL

WELLS CL

ELY WY

P

Football
Ground

CANTERBURY CL

Swimming
Pool

MAP

LOVERIDGE AV

H I L L G R O U N D S

MARSHALL

CHANDLER
PROCTOR CL
EMMER RD

GARDEN CL

FOUNTAIN CL

HARTWELL

MAYFIELD

GDNS

WESTMINSTER GDNS

BUTLER

PRENTICE GDNS

LICHFIELD CL

Hall

6

FOWLER CL

OGILVIE CL

TYNE PENWRTH

STANTON

ADMSON

WILLSHERE

FOSTER RD

KING ST

Kempston
Grange

Grange
School

Clinic

HALSEY RD

ROAD

Addison Howard Park

+

BEDFORD

B531

THORNTON

LITTLEDALE

ROAD

A B C D

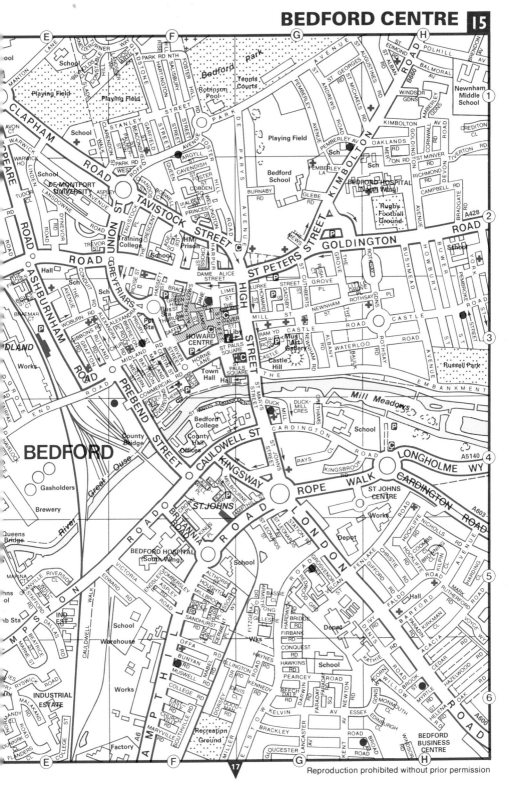

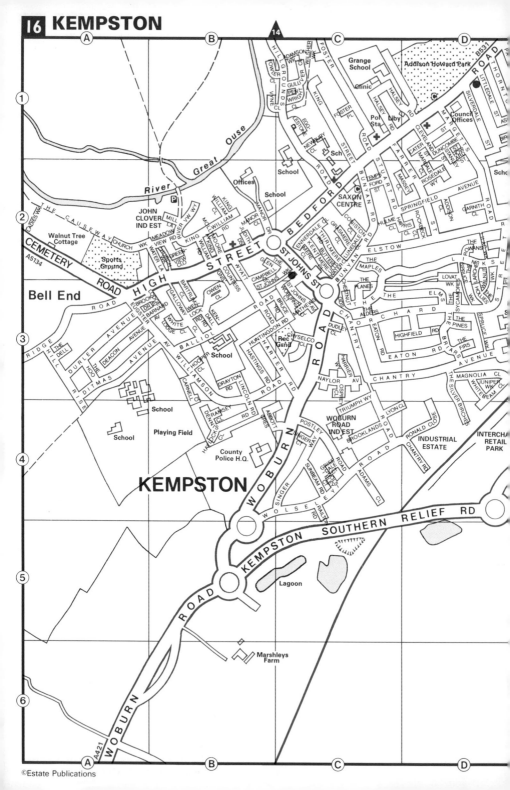

KEMPSTON

Bell End

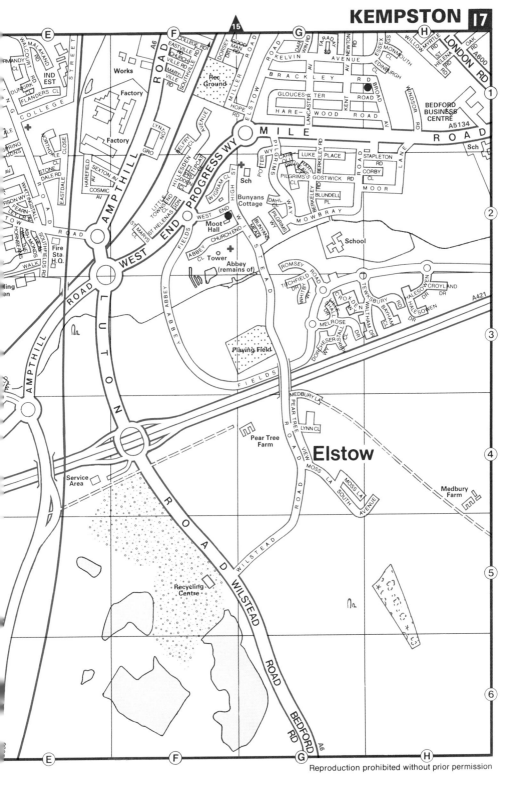

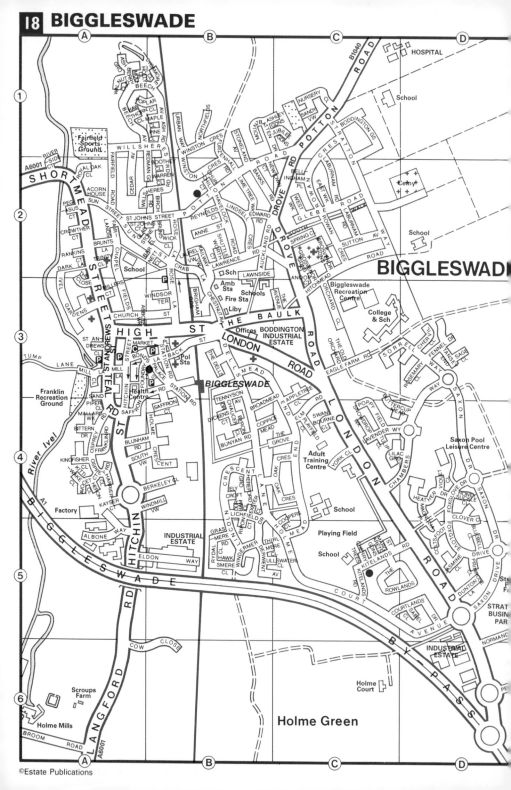

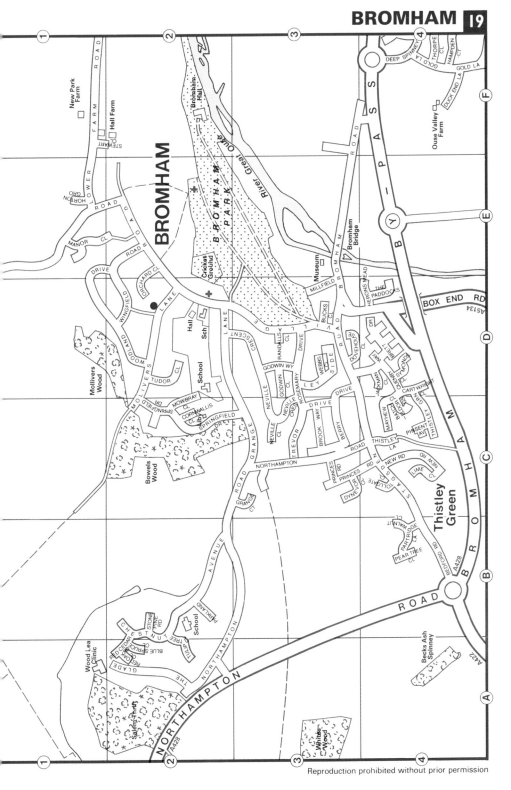

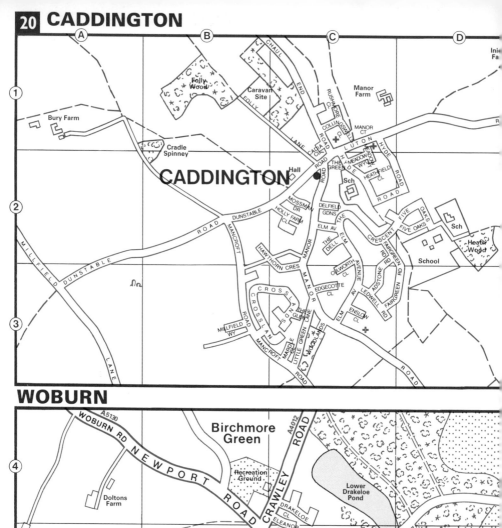

CADDINGTON

Folly Wood

CHAUL END

Caravan Site

Manor Farm

Bury Farm

Cradle Spinney

Hall

Sch

MOSSMAN DR

HOLLY FARM CL

DELFIELD GDNS

FIVE OAKS

Sch

DUNSTABLE

ROAD

MANCROFT

ELM AV

THE DELL

CRESCENT

FIVE OAKS

Heath Wood

MILLFIELD

DUNSTABLE

HAWTHORN CRES

MANOR

CHILWORTH CL

AVENUE

ADSTONE RD

FAIRGREEN RD

School

CROSSLAND

EDGECOTTE CL

LEDWELL RD

MILLFIELD WY

MANCROFT

MARBLE

LITTLE GREEN LANE

WOODLANDS

ENSLOW CL

LANE

ROAD

ROAD

WOBURN

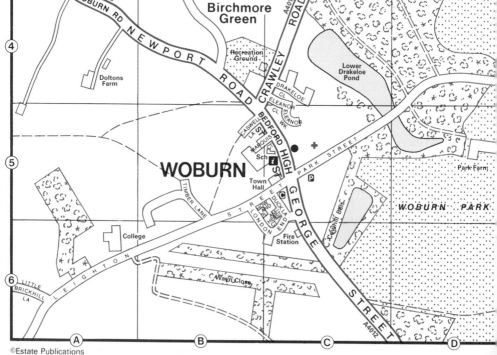

A5130

WOBURN RD

Birchmore Green

A4012 ROAD

NEWPORT ROAD

Recreation Ground

Lower Drakeloe Pond

Doltons Farm

CRAWLEY ROAD

DRAKELOE CL

ELEANOR CL

ELEANOR WK

WOBURN

CASWELL LA

MARQUIS RD

Sch

PARK STREET

Park Farm

BEDFORD ST

Town Hall

HIGH ST

P

TIMBER LANE

College

LONDON

STREET

DUCKLA END

GEORGE STREET

Fire Station

Conihill Belt

WOBURN PARK

LITTLE BRICKHILL LA

LEIGHTON

Wavn Close

A4012

STREET

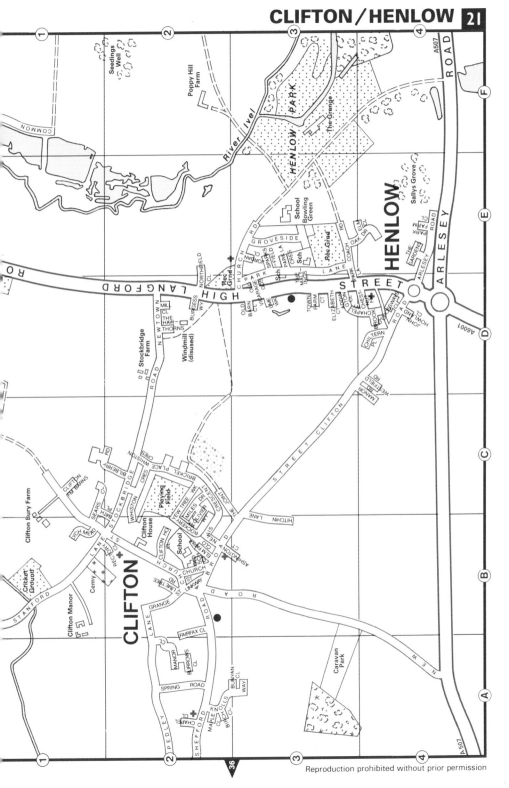

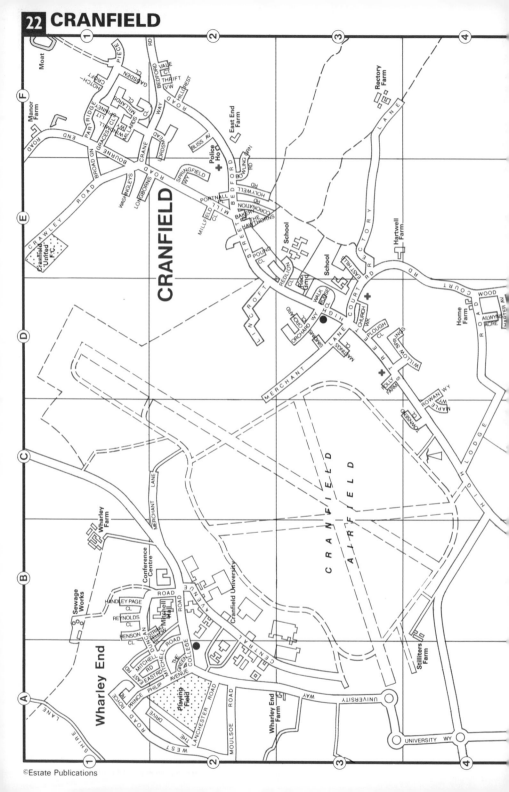

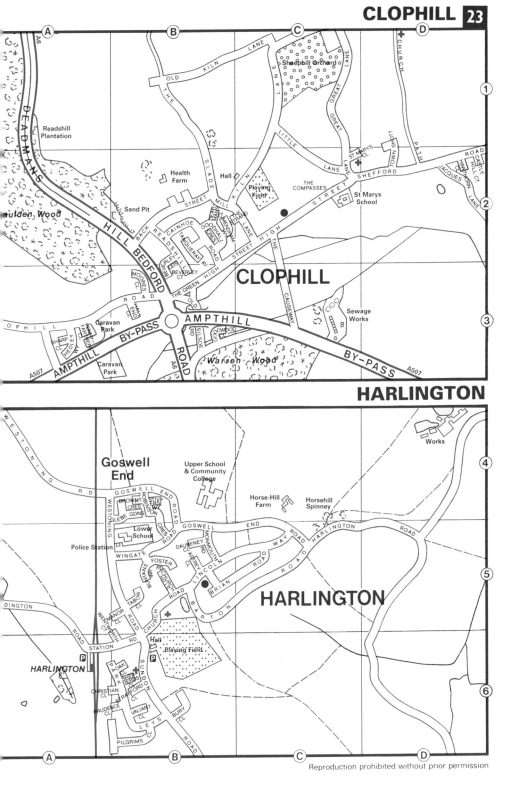

CLOPHILL 23

CLOPHILL

A6 · DEADMANS · Readshill Plantation · aulden Wood · OLD KILN LANE · THE · Sheepbill Orchard · LANE · GREAT · GREAT · CHURCH · Health Farm · Hall · SLADE · STREET · MILL · KILN · Playing Field · THE COMPASSES · LITTLE · LANE · St Marys School · ST MARYS SCHOOL · SHEFFORD · ROAD · CASTLE HILL · HAWTHORN LANE · JACQUES · TOWN SHOTT · PATH · HILL CT · Sand Pit · BACK · READSHILL · CAINHOE · FARQUERAY · GOODHALL · CRES · MENDHAM · ROAD · STREET · HIGH · STREET · THE · HIGH · HILL · BEDFORD · CUST · BEVERLEY · CT · MOORES · CL · THE GREEN · HIGH · ROAD · Caravan Park · OPHILL · SHARP · CL · HEDLEY · AMPTHILL · BY-PASS · OLD · ROAD · AMPTHILL · A507 · Caravan Park · A6 · ROAD · SILSOE · RD · CODWOOD · CL · Warren Wood · CAUSEWAY · Sewage Works · BY-PASS · A507 · CLOPHILL

(1) (2) (3)

HARLINGTON

WESTONING · Works · Goswell End · Upper School & Community College · GOSWELL END ROAD · WESTONING · RD · BROWNS CRES · ROBINSON · STIVY RD · GLEBE GDNS · Lower School · CRES · GOSWELL · END · Horse-Hill Farm · Horsehill Spinney · ROAD · HARLINGTON · ROAD · ROAD · Police Station · WINGATE · FOSTER · DAUBENEY RD · MONMOUTH · OSTREY RD · WAY · ROAD · DINGTON · BUNYANS · RD · CHURCH · LINCOLN · ROAD · TABO · CL · MANOR · ROAD · CL · BRIAN · HARLINGTON · BARTON · CL · WENTWORTH · STATION · RD · CHURCH · HARLINGTON · P · Hall · Playing Field · P · OAK · BEDS · REEDS · CRAWFORD · SUNDON · CHRISTIAN CL · PRUDENCE CL · VALIANT CL · BURY CL · LEYS · ROAD · PILGRIMS

(4) (5) (6)

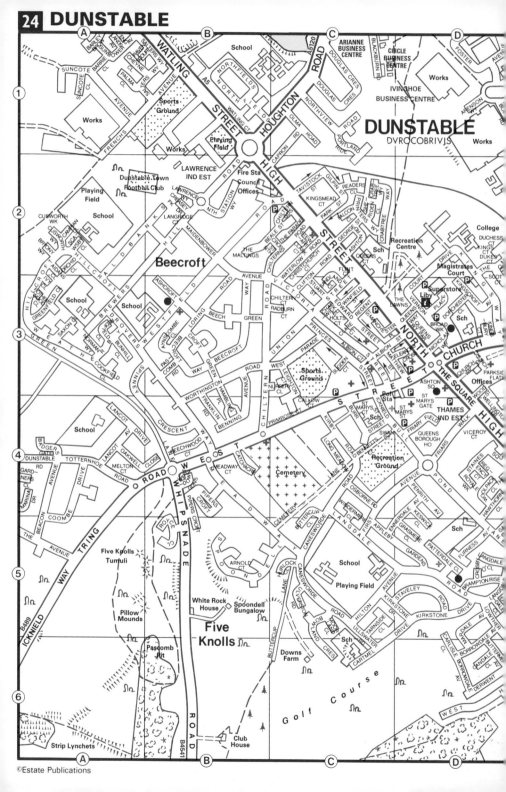

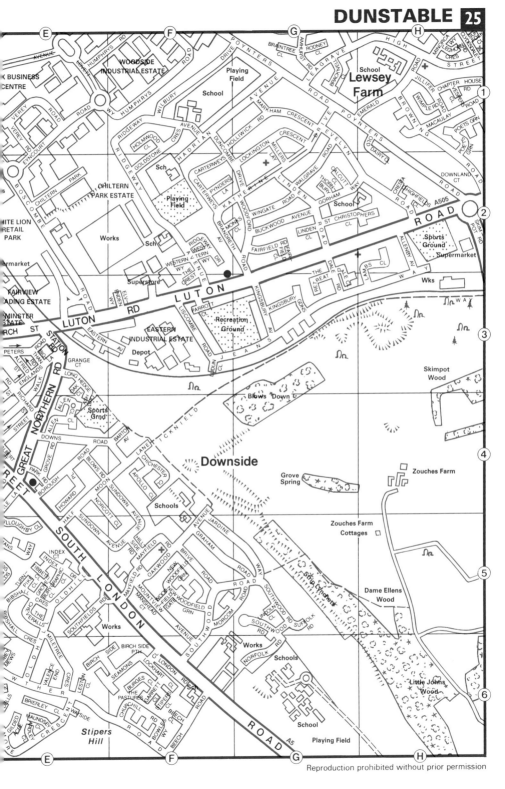

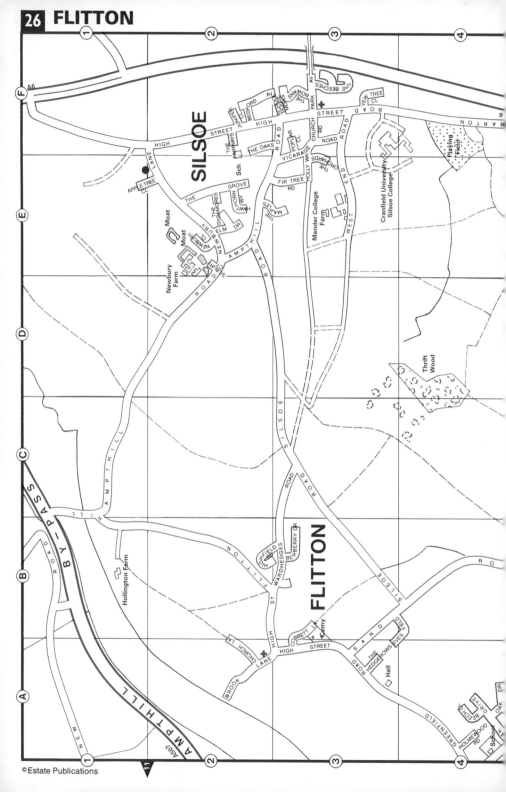

SILSOE

FLITTON

Thrift Wood

Playing Field

Cranfield University Silsoe College

Mander College Farm

Newbury Farm

Moat

Hollington Farm

School

© Estate Publications

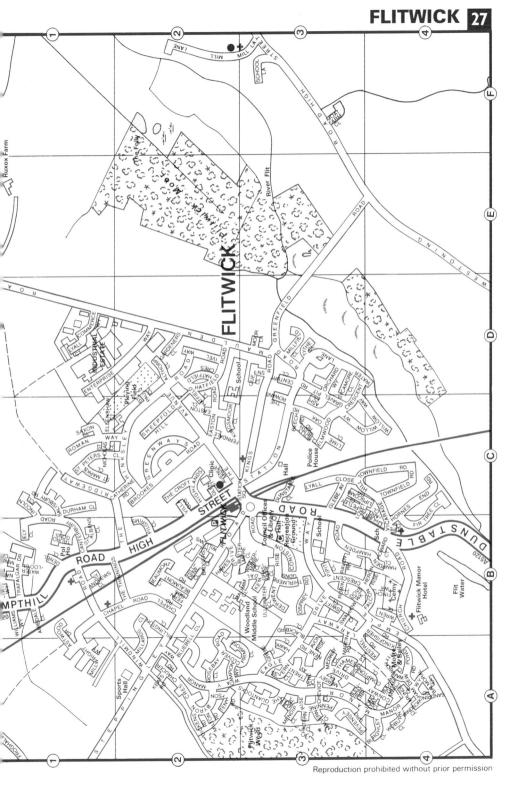

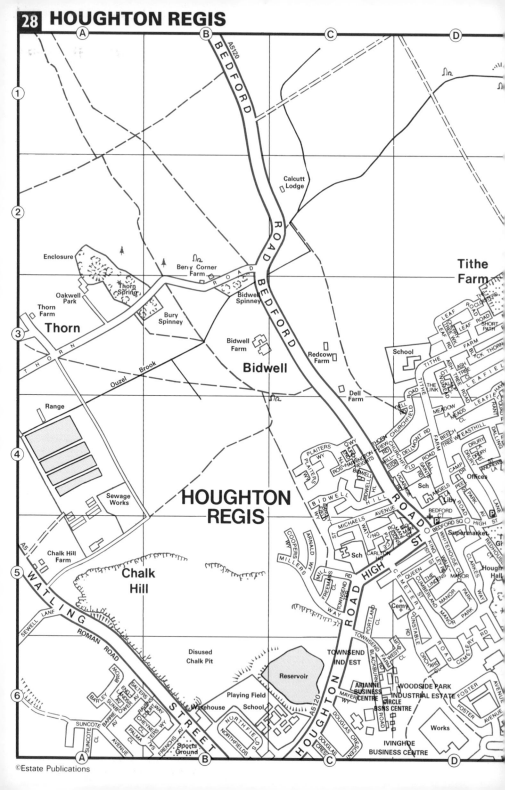

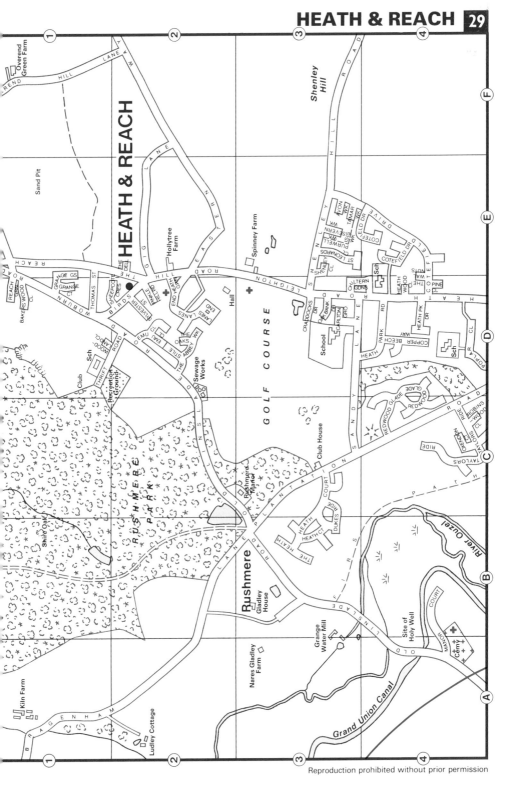

30 LINSLADE

LEIGHTON BUZZARD

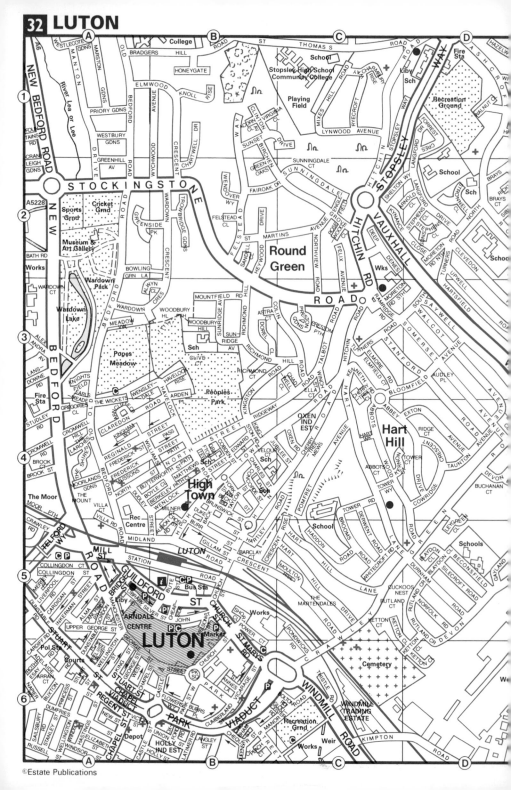

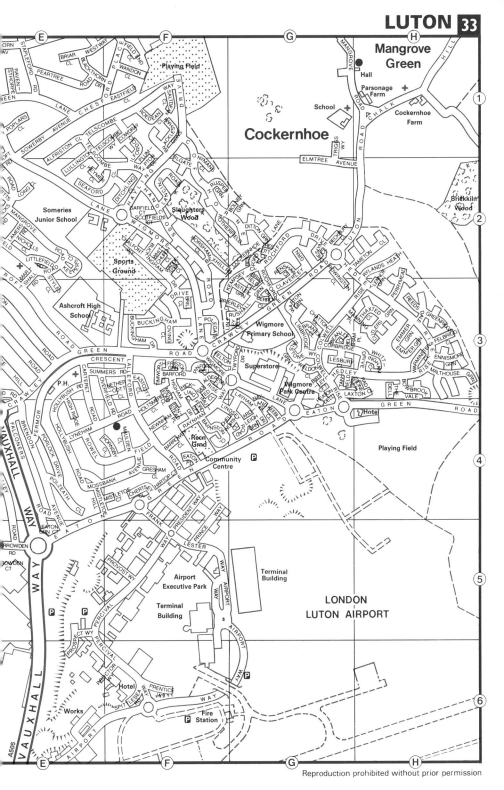

LUTON 33

Mangrove Green

Cockernhoe

LONDON
LUTON AIRPORT

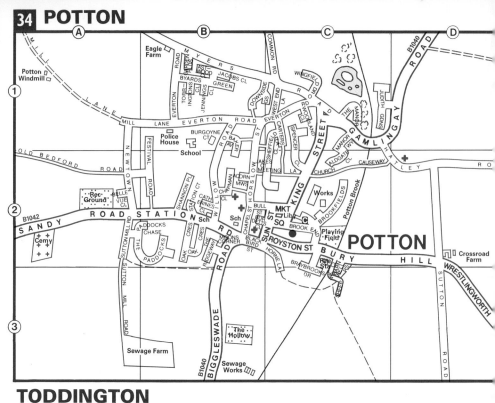

POTTON

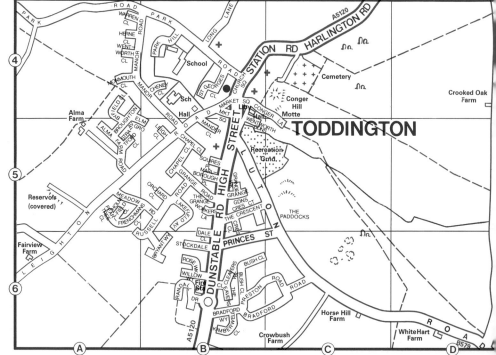

TODDINGTON

©Estate Publications

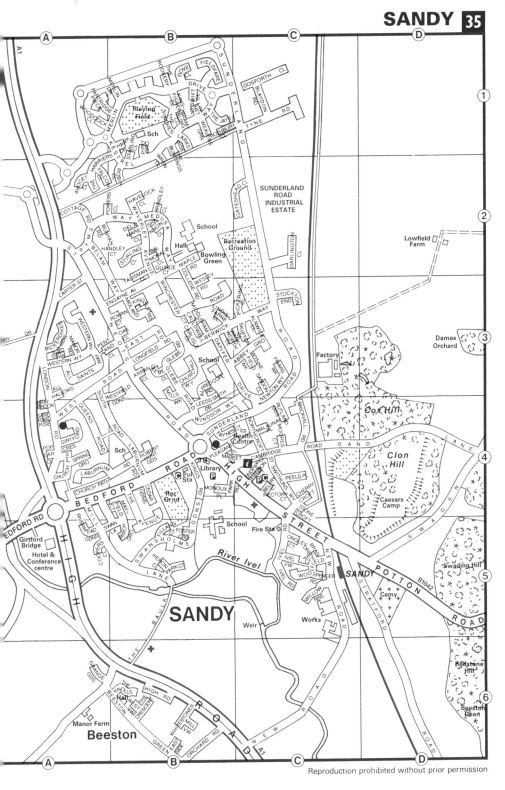

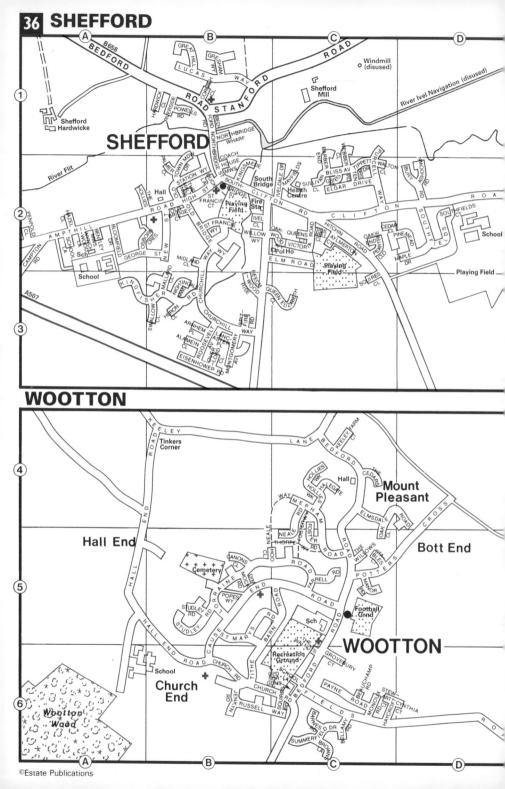

SHEFFORD

WOOTTON

Wootton Wood

Church End

Hall End

Mount Pleasant

Bott End

WOOTTON